The Will and the Way

PAUL R. WILLIAMS, ARCHITECT

To HERRON —

just think . . . !

Karen E. Hudson
26 Feb 94

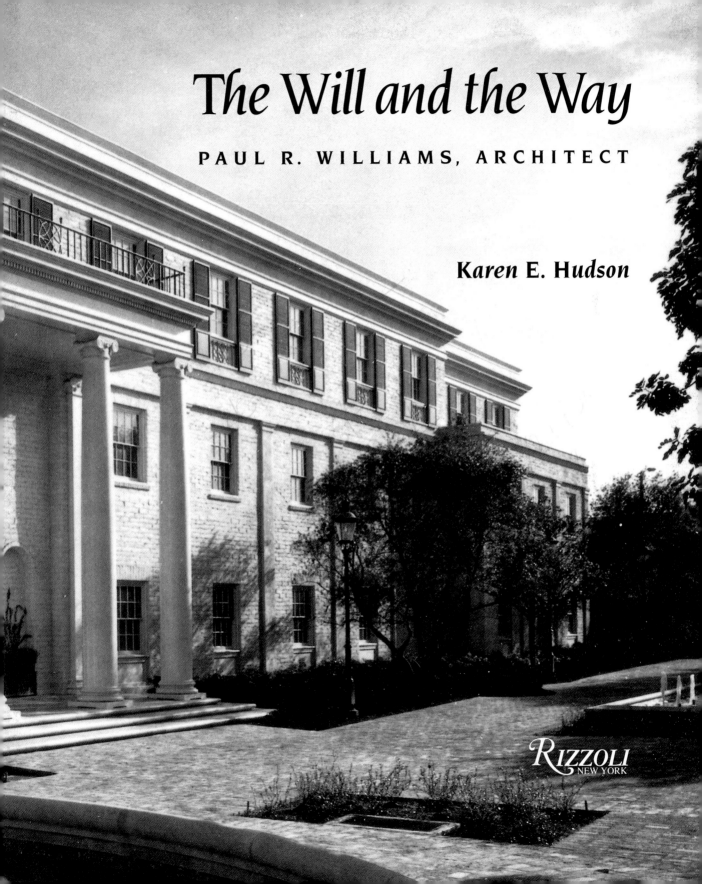

The Will and the Way

PAUL R. WILLIAMS, ARCHITECT

Karen E. Hudson

RIZZOLI
NEW YORK

For my godchildren…
Garth, Alexis, Alyssa, Ariell, and Philip Gregory
—KEH

First published in the United States of America in 1994 by
RIZZOLI INTERNATIONAL PUBLICATIONS, INC.
300 Park Avenue South, New York NY 10010

Library of Congress Number: 93-39986
ISBN: 0-8478-1780-6

Edited by: Kimberly Harbour
Designed by: Christina Bliss

Printed and bound in Singapore

Jacket Front cover: *drawing of Jessie Murphy house;*
photo of Paul Williams at age 28.
Back cover: *Paul Williams, age 71, in front of LAX Airport theme building,*
Los Angeles. Photo by Julius Shulman.
Frontispiece: *Litton Industries, Beverly Hills, California, 1968.*

Introduction

Has anyone ever asked you what you want to be when you grow up? Maybe someone has suggested a road for you to follow. But what if you discovered that the road to your dreams hadn't been built yet?

This is the story of Paul Revere Williams, architect. Paul Williams didn't start out as an architect; he began as a kid, just like the rest of us. As a high school student, he made a commitment to himself to become an architect, and, in 1923, he became the first African-American member of the American Institute of Architects — later the AIA named him a Fellow, a prestigious honor. During a career that spanned nearly sixty years, he designed more than three thousand projects throughout the world — from Canada to Jamaica, Hawaii to Liberia, New York to Colombia, and, of course, in Los Angeles, his home-town. His vision and interests led him to build everything from houses to churches, schools, hospitals, office buildings, and public-housing projects.

Probably the only thing he loved more than architecture was his family. He was a loving husband, father, and — ultimately — a grandfather. That's where I come in. As his granddaughter I learned to wonder about the world around me. And when I grew up I became curious about him, too. I knew Paul Williams — my grandfather — but I knew little about Paul R. Williams, architect. As I uncovered

Williams with grandchildren, Karen and Paul.

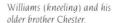
Williams (kneeling) and his older brother Chester.

this side of him, I realized his life was a story that was meant to be shared.

First of all, no biography about Paul Williams would be complete without looking at his childhood, where the roots of the courage and fierce determination he exhibited throughout his life first took hold.

Paul was born on February 18, 1894, in downtown Los Angeles, at Eighth and Santee Streets. His father, Chester; mother, Lila; and brother, Chester, Jr.; had just moved there from Memphis, where his father had been a waiter at the Peabody Hotel. Los Angeles was full of opportunities. Chester, Sr., opened his own fruit stand at the Plaza, which is now known as Olvera Street. When Paul was a toddler he and his mother would walk three blocks to the horsecar to take their daily ride to visit his father's stand. Sadly, Paul's mother and father both died by the time he was four. Orphaned, Paul was raised by loving foster parents, Mr. and Mrs. Clarkson, while Chester, Jr., went to live with another foster family. Even though the brothers weren't able to see each other often, Chester was five years older and made an effort to keep in touch with his little brother.

The Clarksons lived in the neighborhood where Paul was born, so he continued to attend First African Methodist Episcopal Church (First A.M.E.), which is the oldest African-American church in Los Angeles. He was the only African-American in his class at Sentuous Avenue School on Pico Boulevard, where he was known as the class artist; otherwise his childhood experiences were like those of most people in early downtown

Los Angeles. He lived in an integrated neighborhood. After school he and his playmates explored their surroundings. Sometimes they used whiskey-soaked wheat to catch the wild quail that roamed their street. At other times they visited their neighbors. The vegetable man taught them how to conserve natural resources, particularly water. They learned Chinese from the laundryman and German from the new kids who moved to the neighborhood.

His foster father worked as a janitor in a bank at First and Spring Streets. When he was still in elementary school, Paul began selling newspapers on the corner outside the bank to help support the family. Paul sold *The Record* and *The Express*, one for three cents or two for a nickel. U.S. Senator Frank Flint was a regular customer.

Although Paul traveled the world over, Los Angeles remained his home all of his life. Drawing was his lifelong love, too. And, as you will read, First A.M.E. Church and Senator Flint played important roles in his adult life. By holding fast to his dreams and becoming an architect, Paul carved his own road and made it a little easier for more African-American architects to follow. (By 1993, there were 595 African-American members, including forty-two Fellows, in the AIA.)

In 1948, Paul became a grandfather for the first time. It was no small coincidence that his grandson, my brother, was named after him. "Da," as we called our grandfather, left us a legacy through his personal notes, and we know he would be happy that we are sharing them with you. Maybe after reading this book you'll want to take the road to an architectural career — or perhaps you'll decide that you, too, can blaze a new trail. Whatever you choose, remember to celebrate your creativity, learn from the accomplishments of others, and share your knowledge with those who follow.

Karen Elyse Hudson
Director
The Paul R. Williams Collection

Williams and his grandson, Paul Claude.

May 8, 1948

To *my grandson*:

I thought you'd never get here — but finally you've arrived! You should have seen the commotion at the hospital as Claude, your other grandfather, and I anxiously awaited your arrival. You're the first grandchild on both sides of the family. Your parents didn't get a chance to name you, because as soon as Claude and I found out you were a boy, we announced your name to be Paul Claude.

From the moment we heard you were due to join the family, I've kept a special notebook just for you. There's so much I want to tell you, so many experiences I want to share with you. I want you to know I love being an architect. . . . Perhaps you'll be an architect one day yourself. Don't let anyone keep you from achieving your dreams, Paul. You can be whatever you want to be — as long as you have the will and the way.

"How can you, as an individual, fit into this pattern of tomorrow? First, we must be a part of the community in which we live and not apart from it."

"Who ever heard of a Negro being an architect?"

1910–1912

When I was very young I drew pictures of animals. Soon I found myself drawing each building on my route to school. One day a family friend, who was a local builder, said I should become an architect. At the time I wasn't sure what it meant to be one, but I soon found out. I felt like a detective in a dime-store novel, questioning everyone I could about architecture. When I discovered that architects design homes, schools, churches, office buildings — and just about everything imaginable to live and work in — I decided this was the profession for me. Architects also draw the plans of how buildings should be built and supervise their construction. To think that something I drew on a piece of paper would become a building of bricks and boards was nothing less than magical!

When I entered high school the first question the counselor asked me was, "Why do you want to be an architect?" He added, "Why don't you study to be a doctor or a lawyer? Negroes will always need doctors and lawyers, but they build neither fine homes nor expensive office buildings, so you would be obliged to depend entirely on white clients for your livelihood." I told him I had heard of only one Negro architect in America, and I was sure this country could use at least one or two more. (The architect I knew of was Booker T. Washington's son-in-law, William S. Pittman. Of course, there were a few others, but they were back East and I wasn't aware of them.)

My career plans were not well accepted by everyone. Although my family encouraged me at every step, my guidance counselor continued to give me reasons why I would fail. I took architecture courses at Polytechnic High School, but when I told my adviser that I wanted to continue my studies at the university, he stared at me with as much astonishment as he would have had I proposed a rocket flight to Mars! "Who ever heard of a Negro being an architect?" he said.

I suppose it was about 1912 when I made the commitment to become an architect. This was the turning point in my life because I realized I would forever question my right to be all that I could be if I allowed others to discourage me because of the color of my skin. I developed a fierce desire to prove to myself that I could become one of the best architects ever.

I knew I had the will. All I had to do was find the way.

1913–1917

Five years can often seem like a lifetime. But I kept my promise to myself and became an architect. After graduating from high school I enrolled in the Los Angeles Art School and took a job as an architect's helper. The Beaux Arts Institute of Design of New York had a workshop in Los Angeles that accepted me as a student. After three years of study I won the coveted Beaux Arts Medal for excellence in design. Winning this competition reinforced my belief that I would succeed. I realized that the only chance I had of being accepted in the elite world of architecture was to compete on individual merit.

To find a job I went through the yellow pages and copied the addresses of all the architects listed. I arranged them in geographical order, put on my best suit of clothes, and called on each office. I asked if they were hiring or not. Next to each name I wrote down whether the answer was "no" or "maybe next week," and whether it was said with a smile or a frown. The following week I put my sketches in a smart portfolio and went back to each office where someone had smiled. Finally I was offered three positions.

Three dollars per week was the highest salary, and one office paid nothing but gave me the chance to work in one of the most prestigious architectural firms in the city. I knew that this firm would give me invaluable experience, so I took the job. To my surprise they broke their contract and paid me three dollars beginning my very first week.

Shortly thereafter I began working for Wilbur D. Cook, a landscape architect and town planner. My first day in the office I informed the chief draftsman that I was a working drawing man, meaning that I prepared drawings to be used on the job by construction workers. I bluffed my way through the day; then, at night, I took his drawing home and worked until daybreak. I went into the office early the next morning, laid out the drawings on my drafting table, and waited for the chief draftsman to drop by. He was astonished at how quickly I had completed the assignment. Thereafter, he considered me the fastest working drawing man in the office. That's when I decided that I would do things faster, more efficiently, and better than others in order to be judged for my abilities rather than simply dismissed because of the color of my face.

In 1914, when I was twenty, my design for a neighborhood civic center in Pasadena, California, won the first prize of two hundred dollars, beating older and more experienced contestants. I won first honorable mention in architecture at the Chicago Emancipation Celebration in 1915 and the following year placed third for the Sperling Prize, an All-American competition held in New York. It was especially exciting to compete with other architects from across the country, because it's easy to be the best in your town and forget that there's a whole world of competition out there.

I thought drawing ability was all I needed to become an architect, but my boss told me how wrong I was. Even though I had some promising ideas, he explained that I'd never succeed if I only cared about the artistic part. That accounted for only about one quarter of an architect's job. I had not considered how architects obtain commissions to design buildings, only about how thrilling it was to work on them at my drafting board. Once again, my will wasn't enough. I had to find the way.

At the University of Southern California, I enrolled in an engineering program that included business classes. The degree required many math courses, and I was certainly glad I took them. The math helped me make the correct measurements on floor plans and gave me a foundation for the business side of architecture.

Meanwhile, I worked my way through college by making brass U's, S's, and C's for men's watch fobs and women's handbags. At one point five other students worked for me, and I made so much money that I considered changing my mind about school and architecture. Deep down inside, however, I knew the money was temporary and I'd grow bored. Becoming an architect would be a lot of work, but my future depended on staying in school. I took a hard look at my experience (or lack of it) and decided to attend three different art schools for intensive study in interior design, color harmony, and rendering.

With additional education and experience in landscaping under my belt, it was time to find a job that would give me experience in fine home design. I couldn't have asked for a better training ground than working in the offices of Reginald Johnson. Would you believe my first assignment was to design a $150,000 home? Up until then I'd never even been in a home that cost more than $10,000! I couldn't imagine how you could spend so much on a home, but then my employer sent me to look at homes in Santa Barbara, and I soon found out. That trip taught me more than where money was spent; it also taught me how it was spent. The most important lesson I learned was restraint. A room should have a single focal point, regardless of how much money goes into it. If not arranged well, a magnificent collection of furnishings can look like an expensive junk shop. Restraint, then, is a matter of choosing and carefully planning for the total effect.

From that day on my motto became: "Good design is the pleasing assemblage of parts, not the assemblage of pleasing parts." I remember this whenever creative vision is involved. The same idea holds true whether you're getting dressed and putting an outfit together, redecorating your room, or setting the table. It even holds true when selecting people for a committee — it's important to choose people who work well together.

And then there's your grandmother, my Della. We met at First A.M.E. Church, where I was president of Christian Endeavor, an organization for young people who belonged to various churches around town. She attended the Baptist church and enchanted me from the moment I laid eyes on her. We got married in 1917, when I was sure I had a suitable job and was able to provide for her. Being married to Della, and the thought of my own family, meant the world to me. There hasn't been a day yet that if she wanted the moon, I would have not tried to get it for her!

Della Mae Givens Williams, c. 1917.

1925   **LOS ANGELES EXAMINER .... A**

Home Strictly Californian

UNDER the supervision of Paul R. Williams an interesting study for § a San Juan Capistrano residence for the Forster estate has been prepared.

"Being a Californian was to my advantage. In California
the people are interested in ideas that are new and fresh without the
traditional or historical ties that are ordinarily more associated
with East Coast thinking."

Starting a Practice

1918–1923

By 1919, I became somewhat of a specialist in designing small homes — a skill that did not go unnoticed by my young bride. I was working all of the time, and Della decided it was time for us to find our own home. She found the house and assured the real estate agent that we'd have the down payment in no time. I had been too preoccupied with work to consider entering any of the ongoing architectural contests. Your grandmother, on the other hand, was determined to get that down payment and persuaded me to enter three contests at once. I won all three and earned enough money for the down payment. We moved into our new home within a few weeks.

It was an exciting time. I was becoming involved in city politics. In 1920, I was appointed to the first Los Angeles City Planning Commission, where I looked forward to shaping our growing city. At this point in my career I felt I should gain experience in designing large, public buildings, so I went to work for John C. Austin. During the three years I worked with Austin, his firm designed and built about thirty schools. I also helped prepare construction drawings for the Shrine Auditorium, the Chamber of Commerce, and the First Methodist Church of Los Angeles.

In 1921, I obtained my license to practice architecture in California. My dreams were finally being realized.

One day a high school buddy of mine, Louis Cass, looked me up and asked if I was interested in designing his new home in the hills of Flintridge. Flintridge was a new development that had been started by the same Senator Frank Flint to whom I sold newspapers. When Senator Flint asked me to design a number of homes in his new development, he was shocked to find out I was that same little newspaper boy. Luckily, he remembered I was a reliable and hard worker.

Building the Cass Home gave me the money I needed to open my own office in late 1922. I secured a garden suite on the roof of the stock exchange building, and Paul R. Williams, Architect, became an official business. In 1923, I joined the Southern California Chapter of the American Institute of Architects (AIA) becoming the national organization's first Negro member. My business began to prosper. Each day I met with some of the most exciting leaders in the community, who began to accept me as a friend and often offered to include me in their business dealings. I'll never forget the time I was supervising a new home for Motley Flint, vice president of Pacific Southwest Trust and Savings Bank. This particular afternoon he was two hours late for his appointment with me. When he finally arrived, he was very excited because he had just left a board meeting where they had bought the rights for the first talking motion picture. He said, "Paul, can you get together $500 by tomorrow?"

"Sorry, my wife wants a new house," I told him. Can you imagine? That patent controlled talking motion pictures for the next ten years!

1924–1927

By now my practice included more than just homes. I thought about my high school counselor, who had been sure I wouldn't get any jobs within the Negro community, when I designed the Second Baptist Church and the Connor-Johnson Mortuary, which was built entirely by Negro craftsmen. We also designed the Hostetter Elementary School,

Opposite: *Second Baptist Church, Los Angeles, 1924.*

Left:
The Twenty-eighth Street YMCA was built for "colored boys." Over the course of history, Americans of African descent have been referred to by various names. In the 1920s, African-Americans were called "colored." In the 1930s, they were called "Negroes." And, by the 1960s, the Black Power Movement popularized the term "Blacks." Currently "African-American" is used.

Opposite:
Frederick Douglass, as shown in the upper left facade of the Twenty-eighth Street YMCA.

the Twenty-eighth Street YMCA, and the Hollywood YMCA. The Twenty-eighth Street YMCA was the first YMCA in Los Angeles for "colored boys and young men." I had grown up going to the Ninth Street YMCA — twenty blocks away — and knew how badly we needed one in our community. I also knew how important it was for young people to have role models, so I incorporated likenesses of the abolitionist Frederick Douglass and educator Booker T. Washington into the ornate design on the facade of the building.

Los Angeles grew as many people, particularly in the entertainment industry, moved West. Samuel Goldwyn and Louis B. Mayer formed Metro-

Goldwyn-Mayer Film Studio, Harry Cohn founded Columbia Pictures, and, in radio, the National Broadcasting Corporation (NBC) and Columbia Broadcasting System (CBS) got their starts. Coming from crowded New York City, these new Angelenos found the open fields of Beverly Hills an invitation to build new homes. And guess who wanted to be their architect?

*"To be sincere in my work, I must design homes, not houses.
I must take into consideration each family's mode of living, its present
economic problems, and its probable economic future."*

Building Beverly Hills

1928–1929

The demand for Paul Williams' designs continued over the next couple of years. Actors as well as new studio heads came to me for their homes. After I did a home for Lon Chaney, Sr., he asked that I design a "rockhouse" weekend home for him and his wife. Later, the rockhouse was used in the film *Man of a Thousand Faces*, which was about Chaney's life. Nineteen twenty-eight also found me in the Hollywood Hills, designing a home for Victor Rossetti, the president of Farmer's and Merchants Bank; in Santa Monica, for the design of a drive-in market; and even in Phoenix, Arizona, doing a home for the Korrick family. I had already designed over a dozen homes in Flintridge, and there were more to come. But nothing captured my imagination as much as my commission to design an English Tudor estate for racehorse owner Jack Atkin — "Overcoat Jack," as he liked to be called.

Atkin had fond memories of his childhood in England and wanted a home that reminded him of his youth. I worked extra hard on the drawings. The home was estimated to cost $350,000, and Atkin approved of everything but the price. I thought I'd have to cut back on some of the details to lower the price, but that wasn't the problem. Overcoat Jack had already told all of his buddies at the racetrack that his new home was going to cost a half million dollars. I had to add $150,000 to the home! In 1929, during the Great Depression, it wasn't easy to add that much, but I struggled and made it (smile). That's the kind of client you like to have! One of the best things about being an architect is having fun spending other people's money.

Opposite: *Lon Chaney Residence, Beverly Hills, California, 1929.*

Jack P. Atkin Residence, Pasadena, California, 1929. Atkin lived in the home with his wife, daughter, and staff of fourteen.

Atkin's home was used for many movies — including the original *Topper* — and the studios paid him well for renting it as a location. Atkin donated his film earnings to the soup kitchens to feed poor people in Pasadena. I always liked him — he told great stories about the racetrack, but more importantly, he gave something back to his community.

1930 –1932

By now we had two little girls, Norma and Marilyn (your mother). There was never a spare moment. The office attracted nothing less than breathtaking projects. In 1931, I designed two Mediterranean homes that remained among my favorites. One was a home for Fred Price, in the Palisades above Pacific Coast Highway. The other was for a Swiss engineer named John Zublin, built in the Bel Air section of Los Angeles. The Price home was a challenge because it was perched high on a cliff overlooking the Pacific Ocean. The Zublin home was rather simple from the front, but inside it had painted ceilings, wrought-iron staircases, and a ballroom — complete with a stage — tucked into the lower level.

Hillsides always presented a particular challenge — and everyone wanted a swimming pool. Zublin couldn't swim, but he wanted one, too. He figured he could paddle his canoe in the pool without drowning as long as he could touch the sides with his oars. So I planned a narrow, 300-foot-long pool that was carved into the hillside. It would have been much simpler if Zublin had learned to swim!

With his engineering skills, Zublin worked with me to develop a series of waterfalls and rock formations instead of the usual grass and flowers in the backyard. It was not unusual for a client to make suggestions for special features to be incorporated in the design of a home. For example, E. L. Cord, the eccentric auto manufacturer, was involved in every stage of building his home.

When I first met Cord I thought he might be prejudiced, so I thought of a way to overcome this. Once, he telephoned and informed me — in a very abrupt way — that he had acquired a property in Beverly Hills and intended to build a new residence. He asked if I would meet him at the site immediately to discuss some ideas. I tried to put him off until the next day but finally gave in. Based on our telephone conversation, I could tell he valued prompt action. After we looked over the site, the land on which he planned to build, he demanded to know when I would have preliminary drawings ready for him, adding that he had already discussed plans with other architects. "By four o'clock tomorrow afternoon," I answered. "Why, that's impossible," he cried. "Every other architect has asked for two or three weeks." He stared at me for a few minutes and then said, "Go ahead."

I delivered those preliminary plans by four o'clock the next day, as promised. (I didn't tell him that I had worked for twenty-two hours, without eating or sleeping. Sometimes that's what you have to do.) Cord gave me the job, and together we worked out the possibilities. Most of the homes I designed at the time were less than 3,200 square feet. His home was ten times that size, with fifteen bedrooms. He gave me a free hand to execute every detail as I saw fit. Craftsmen from Cord's auto-manufacturing business actually built most of the fixtures.

Cord's home became the "showplace" of Beverly Hills. The Cords loved to give parties, and in no time everyone in Beverly Hills had seen my most magnificent creation. After that, I never experienced a shortage of business.

Cars were a passion of mine, and my cream-colored Cord was always my favorite. Now that I think about it, I taught your mother to drive in that car!

From Model T's to Lincoln Continentals, Williams loved cars. This car took him to Pasadena and Flintridge to supervise construction of his buildings.

Left: E. L. Cord Residence,
main entrance, 1931.
This drawing, below, details
how to build the staircase,
which is shown in its
final form, right.

*"From the moment when the first sketch is conceived until
the day when the building stands complete, there is, of necessity,
a close bond between client and architect."*

Success Builds on Success

1933–1939

One of the fringe benefits of being an architect is exchanging ideas with some of the most innovative thinkers in the country. During the early 1930s, my client list grew and I met or worked with experts in every imaginable field. I had the privilege of designing homes for Jay Paley of CBS; Leon Schlesinger, the creator of Looney Toon cartoons; Moshe Menuhin, father of the musical prodigy, Yehudi Menuhin; and Thomas Hamilton of Hamilton Beech appliances.

Meanwhile, one job led to another — like when Cord was visiting his friend Adam Gimbel in New York. Gimbel wanted to open a department store in Beverly Hills that would make customers feel as if they were in an elegant home. Of course, I was the man for the job. Cord told Gimbel that and then called me, saying, "Come to New York in the morning. I've got a job for you." Of course I went. The store was Saks Fifth Avenue. Gimbel hired me to design the interiors of the original building, while the team of Parkinson and Parkinson designed the exterior. Within a year, construction began on two additions, and this time I was hired to design both the exteriors and interiors.

Maynard Parker

Fur Salon, opposite, and Sweater Bar, above, Saks Fifth Avenue, Beverly Hills, California, 1939.

31

Some architects like designing just the exterior of buildings because that's what everyone sees. I like designing both. After all, interiors are more important to the people inside the buildings. Part of my job as an architect is to create a pleasant environment for people to live and work in.

Although I was thrilled to have so many opportunities to design mansions, I was always concerned about affordable housing for those less fortunate. In 1936, after becoming licensed to practice in Washington, D.C., I established an office with Hilyard Robinson, a successful Washington-based architect. Our initial joint venture (along with an architect by the name of Porter) was to design Langston Terrace, the first federally-funded public housing project in the country.

As I sketched plans for large country homes in the most beautiful places in the world, sometimes I dreamed of living there. I could afford such a home, but each evening, I returned to my small home in a restricted area of Los Angeles where Negroes were allowed to live. I could not forget that I was not accepted the way other architects were. For example, when I visited my Washington, D.C., office to supervise work being done there, I took the train. If I traveled through the South I rode in the "Jim Crow" car. The seats were no less comfortable than those in any other car, but riding there was a constant reminder that people who had never met me disliked me just because of the color of my skin. If I traveled through the North and stopped in certain hotels, tried to dine in certain restaurants, or even sat beside certain persons on a crowded streetcar, there was a good chance I could cause an "embarrassing situation," not because of what I might say or do, but because of what I looked like.

It was during times like these that I remembered the words of my friend and mentor, Ernest Holmes, who taught me to believe in myself and always to think positively. A minister, Holmes once said: "Failure is only a temporary stop in making a probability a possibility." If you, my grandson, can keep this thought in mind, you, too, will have less difficulty facing life's challenges.

Opposite: *Pool house and pool showing zodiac design, Jay Paley Residence, Bel Air, California, 1934.*

1940–1942

Jobs often came from totally unexpected places. A group of South American businessmen came to the United States looking for an architect to design a new hotel in Colombia. Because the climates in Southern California and South America are similar, they thought the California style of architecture would work well in Colombia. The businessmen selected five homes and asked who designed each one. I had designed three of the five, so they automatically offered me the job. I brushed up on my Spanish, headed for South America, and opened an office in Bogotá.

We began a number of projects in Bogotá and Medellin. I particularly enjoyed working on Sr. Luis Tores' home and the Hotel Granada. Life was very different in Colombia, however. For example, Medellin lay in a rich agricultural district and blossomed into an industrial city, yet it still had some simple — though effective — customs. One time I visited a big meat market in the center of the city, which covered an entire city block and was all fenced and wired in; you could enter through only four doors, one on each side of the block. While I was looking around, I heard a terrific shouting and saw people scampering around on the far side of the market. Then a bell began ringing, and all four doors automatically slammed shut. I couldn't figure out what was going on until someone turned to me and said, "Just another thief." They slammed the doors shut, trapping everyone inside, and hunted the thieves at their leisure.

Hotel commissions began coming my way in this country, too. The Arrowhead Springs Hotel, built in association with Gordan Kaufmann, was a large project but not without my trademark touches. I love curves, and you can't miss them in that swimming pool.

Opposite: *Hotel Granada, Bogotá, Colombia.*

Arrowhead Springs Hotel, above, and its dining room, Arrowhead Springs, California, 1940.

Maynard Parker

36

We broke ground on the Pueblo del Rio Housing Project here in Los Angeles, and I began working for the U.S. Navy as part of the World War II effort. I closed my office and relocated it to my home. It was a difficult time. Home construction was put on hold because all surplus materials and resources went to help fight the war. Each day was an unknown. During this time I had Navy projects and various smaller jobs that kept me busy.

In one ironic twist, a home that I designed for Jessie Murphy in the Pacific Palisades was taken over by the U.S. military. The client commissioned me to build a self-contained compound with separate buildings to house generators, farm animals, vegetable gardens, a dairy, and a laundry so that a number of people could live there for up to a year. We completed only the outer service buildings. Then the FBI received a tip and arrested the German couple who lived there. They were spies, using radio equipment to send signals to their German, anti-American friends. Can you imagine? I had no idea this was going on. I was simply caught up in designing an exquisite 40,000-square-foot home!

Pueblo del Rio Housing Project, Los Angeles, 1941.

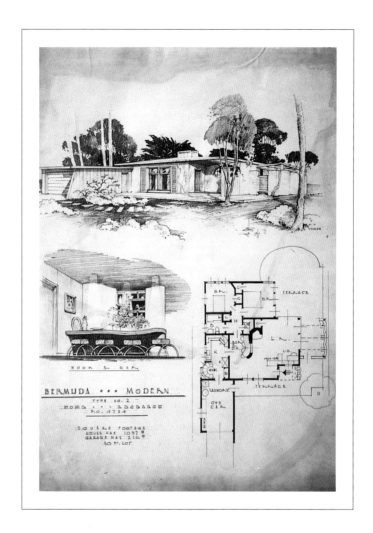

BERMUDA ••• MODERN

"There is also the matter of style versus design. Design concerns itself with the overall formal solution to a problem of building. But buildings, too, must wear style that will give them an association to a certain period of time. How carefully the architect balances the elements in his work, to a good degree, determines the stature attained by him in his profession."

The Postwar Architect

1943–1949

After the war there was greater emphasis on technology and on modern styles of building. I couldn't wait to be a part of it. One particular home I designed had a turntable for the car in the driveway. The wife, who wasn't very skilled at backing the car out, had only to turn the turntable around and drive the car out straight. This worked much the way they turn cable cars around in San Francisco. At the same time, as military personnel returned from the war and residential building resumed, I realized how difficult it was for a young family starting out to afford their dream home. With them in mind, I wrote two books on small homes: *The Small Home of Tomorrow* and *New Homes for Today*.

As an architect in postwar America I bridged the gap between the traditional designs of the previous decade and the modern styles, but there had been little, if any, change in the attitudes toward Negroes. For example, the Ritts family came from Oklahoma to ask me to design a summer home for them at Lake Chautauqua, New York. Mrs. Ritts told me that she fretted all the way out because she had never had to shake a Negro man's hand and wasn't sure how to behave! Once I put her at ease we got along famously. Long ago I perfected some

*Cover and sample page (opposite),
Paul Williams' book,
The Small Home of
Tomorrow, 1945.*

39

marketing tricks to make my clients feel more comfortable. One of the most effective was drawing upside down. If I had the slightest notion that my clients might be uncomfortable being in close contact with me, such as sitting on the same side of the desk, I sat across the table from them and asked questions about their new home. I would ask if they entertained at home or in a hotel, and if they preferred having parties in a formal living room or a comfortable family room. As they shared their ideas, I sketched upside down so their ideas would come alive—right side up—before their eyes. They became full partners in the vision at its earliest stage.

But the most exciting time in 1946 was the marriage of your parents. Your father, Elbert, had just returned from overseas and was the son of my good friend, Dr. H. Claude Hudson. My being an architect came in handy for

H. Claude Hudson, Elbert and Marilyn Williams Hudson, and Della and Paul Williams, at Elbert and Marilyn's wedding, 1946.

The Beverly Hills Hotel, Beverly Hills, California, 1949, home of the Williams' Polo Lounge design.

the family. I designed a special altar for the church where your mom and dad were married, First A.M.E. It wasn't long before your father became like a son to your grandmother and me.

Then, in 1947, your grandfather Claude asked me to join him on the board of directors of Broadway Federal Savings and Loan, which had just opened. I was happy to serve on the board. For too long white-owned banks had kept Negroes and other minorities from getting home loans, a practice called redlining. I spent my entire adult life designing homes for others and believed that the survival of a community depended on homeownership. I desperately wanted Negroes to be able to own their own homes.

The glamour was back in Hollywood, and I was thrilled to be a part of it as my office bristled with steady commissions. I began work on a new wing

of the Beverly Hills Hotel and a major remodel of the interior of the main building. I had a feeling that The Polo Lounge and Fountain Coffee Shop would become landmarks. Yet once again I found myself designing places that would not welcome me had I not been Paul Williams, architect. Some things change, some things remain the same.

Changes were beginning to take place in all walks of life. In 1947, Jackie Robinson became the first Negro major-league baseball player by signing with the Brooklyn Dodgers. A couple of years earlier Supervisor Leonard Roach "broke the ice" and helped me win the assignment to design a unit of Los Angeles General Hospital, making me the first Negro person commissioned to design a large, public building in Los Angeles County.

Opposite: *The Ambassador Hotel coffee shop, Los Angeles, 1949, featuring Williams' signature curves.*

Right: *Williams, second from left, shows a model of the Golden State Building (1948) to insurance executives, from left, Edgar Johnson, Norman Houston, and George Beavers. Founded in 1925, this was the first African-American insurance company in Los Angeles.*

1950–1953

The year 1950 was a big one for the family. While you and your parents stayed home and awaited the arrival of your baby sister, Karen, your grandmother and Aunt Norma joined me for a trip to Europe. I was an associate architect on the United Nations Building in Paris, and the trip confirmed my belief that my work was my "fun." A few weeks later, as we awaited our train from Italy to Switzerland, we discovered we'd misplaced our tickets and had already converted our money and had no Italian lire. Overhearing the conversation, an elderly woman approached and asked, "Aren't you the American architect Paul Williams?" She went on to tell me that she lived at the Beverly Hills Hotel and was very happy there. She told us she'd be honored to have her secretary take care of the tickets, and we could repay her when we returned to Los Angeles. The kindness of people who live in my designs has always overwhelmed me.

In 1951, I moved the office to another building on Wilshire Boulevard and found myself managing a staff of fifty-one. Finally, our new dream home was complete, and Della and I moved in. As you must know by now, your grandmother runs the house. She wanted everything designed especially for our way of living, so in addition to designing the house, I also drew the plans for all of the furniture and had it custom built. Once the house was ready and furnished, Della just walked out of our old home and left all our old furniture behind. It was terrific walking into a house where everything was brand-new and waiting to be used.

I was still a perfectionist and tended to every detail. It was never enough to simply design a building; I tried to be involved in the landscaping, too. Such was the case with the renovation of the El Mirador Hotel in Palm Springs, an old hotel that was converted to an army hospital during the war. The owners hired me to change the hospital into an up-to-date hotel. I wanted the hotel to recapture its original resort atmosphere, so I decided the grounds needed some new palm trees. Elbert, your dad, drove me down to a tree farm in Indio, near San Diego, and I personally selected each palm tree. The workers removed them, and took them back to Palm Springs, where I directed how to plant each tree. It was time-consuming, but I achieved the desired effect.

Your father was terrific. He often drove me from place to place during that time, particularly to Palm Springs. I had a number of projects going on there at one time, including a weekend home for Lucille Ball and Desi Arnaz.

One of the highlights of the year — and of my career — was winning the Spingarn Medal. The National Association for the Advancement of Colored People awards the medal each year to the Negro who has accomplished the most in his or her field. I was very honored that the NAACP recognized me. The regular history books may never be interested in my accomplishments, but I know I will be recognized in Negro history journals if only for having won the Spingarn Medal.

Paul and Della Williams' home, Los Angeles, 1951.

Adams Studio

"Planning is thinking beforehand how something is to be made or done, and mixing imagination with the product — which in the broad sense makes all of us planners. The only difference is that some people get a license to get paid for thinking and the rest of us just contribute our good thoughts to our fellow man."

National Recognition

1954–1955

For weeks all we talked about was our trip to the White House. We attended a state dinner in honor of President Magloire of Haiti. I thought, as an architect, I was the one in the family who appreciated details, but your grandmother didn't miss a thing! She even consulted Emily Post to determine whether or not to remove her evening gloves when being introduced to President and Mrs. Eisenhower. After a wonderful dinner, the women retired to one room and the men to another. Later all of us enjoyed a concert featuring Marian Anderson, who sang beautifully. We were so proud. It was an unforgettable evening.

During the early 1950s, we spent a lot of time at our weekend retreat at Lake Elsinore. It was wonderful to get away from the city and all the pressures of work. I had begun to do many more commercial buildings than individual homes. As I mentioned, most architects had abandoned the conservative historic styles of my early practice, but every once in a while a new client would request a colonial home. One client, Mrs. Landis, said all of her friends had tried to talk her into getting a modern home. But she said she'd waited all her married life to get a Paul Williams colonial, and that was what she was going to get!

Building styles change with time and fashion, but I measure my worth as an architect by my ability to please my client. Each home I design has something special and different from anyone else's home, but I've never made a house so trendy that, when the owners wanted to move, no one else would be interested in buying it.

Opposite: *Paul and Della as they leave home for trip to White House, 1955.*

1956–1957

Work began on the new Los Angeles Airport, where I helped create the signature building. I never seemed to have time to play tennis, but I always made time for my grandchildren. I wanted you to enjoy the creative process as much as I did, maybe that's why I was always buying you the latest mechanical toys. You and Karen were finally at an age that made buying you toys almost as much fun for me as it was for you. My favorite store was F.A.O. Schwarz in New York. I never tired of gadgets and was fascinated by all kinds of mechanical toys. I'll never forget the look on your faces when the puppet theater and roller coaster arrived. Every kid on the block was lined up to ride the roller coaster as it wound around the backyard. It was only two or three feet off the ground, but I think I finally found the ultimate "grandkids" gift. Being a grandfather was the greatest!

You're never too old to learn something new. No matter how diligently I tried to plan ahead and anticipate design problems, I never stopped learning. Sometimes the lesson learned is in reverse, after a building is built. Once, I was riding in the club car on the way to Florida when we passed a large cotton mill. The gentleman sitting next to me knew I was an architect and said, "Passing the mill reminds me of an incident that I think would be of interest to you. I own two cotton mills in the South. One of these is very successful, and the other was a problem and always giving us trouble. The yarn produced from the looms was not consistent in diameter, and this would only happen a few days — or maybe a few minutes — each week; consequently, much of the yardage was ruined and had to be thrown out. We called a number of experts, with no results. As usual, when we closely watched the loom it behaved perfectly. Then one day a Negro maintenance man told the manager he thought he could solve the problem. We gave him the opportunity. All he did was paint the windows on the south side of the factory. His explanation was that as the sun would

Los Angeles International Airport
Theme Building, which was designed
in association with Periera & Luckman
and Welton Becket and Associates.

Vanguard Photography

shine on the looms — about fifteen minutes each day — it caused the cotton to expand because it had been treated with a gloss chemical." This solved the problem and the next factory was built with north windows only. The factory owner paid the "planner" a generous reward.

In 1957, a milestone in my career occurred: I was elected to the honor society of the AIA, being named to the College of Fellows. I was the first Negro so honored.

*"Good architecture should reduce human tension
by creating a restful environment and changing social patterns."*

Giving Something Back

1961

Nineteen sixty-one found me spending more and more afternoons sitting around with actor Danny Thomas, discussing our visions for the future and for children. Danny wanted to build a hospital in Memphis, Tennessee, for children from all walks of life. The more he talked, the more interested I became. One night I dreamed about the new hospital and envisioned it in the shape of a star. Next thing I knew, I was as caught up in the excitement as Danny was. He didn't have much money to get started, and I was proud to donate my services just to be a part of his dream. There are some projects, some friendships, that are more important than the amount of money they earn you. St. Jude Hospital was one such project.

That year, fire raged through Bel Air and destroyed over 400 homes; some were ones I had designed. I've been known to get kind of attached to my designs, but I realize that they are only buildings and can be rebuilt. I'm just grateful the families who lived in them were unharmed. It reminds me how very fragile our everyday lives are and of the importance of family and friends.

Opposite: *First A.M.E. Church, Los Angeles, 1964.*
Right: *St. Jude Hospital, Memphis, Tennessee, 1962.*

1964

The summer of 1964, between your sophomore and junior years in high school, you worked for me. As I recall, your biggest project was to measure out parking spaces for the Pasadena Fedco store. I'm afraid you didn't seem that interested in architecture. Broadway Federal's new Midtown office was also on our drawing boards that year. I began to think that perhaps you'd follow in the footsteps of Claude and your father and become a lawyer and head Broadway Federal. No matter what you decide to become, you must remember three things: Read, read, read! Claude and I may not have been typical grandfathers, but like all grandfathers we have always wanted the best for you. Even though we have been tempted to influence you, we want you to choose your own road and become whatever you want to be. We don't know what you'll finally do with your life, but at least we know you love swimming and tennis just as we do.

The year ended with my office beginning work on the new First A.M.E. Church, and the Assistance League building was completed, giving a wonderful old organization a graceful new setting.

1966

Well, Paul, you graduated from high school and headed off to Berkeley. I guess it's safe to say you're not interested in architecture. Your sister Karen has celebrated her "sweet sixteen." I asked her what she wanted for her birthday, and naturally she wanted me to design her dream house. I explained to her that she had to have the site selected first — I needed to know if the home would be placed on a hill or flat land, where the trees were, and the direction the sun rose in the morning. I always design homes with breakfast rooms facing the morning sun. Karen wasn't thrilled with my response. Maybe she'll settle for a charm bracelet.

H. Claude Hudson and Paul Williams at Karen's "Sweet Sixteen" party.

Fitzgerald Whitney

1967–1973

Because of my diabetes, my eyesight has deteriorated and prevents me from writing as often as I'd like. The disease never kept me down until it began to affect my eyes. When your whole world revolves around the appreciation of beautiful things and details, it's disheartening to view it less clearly. I don't drive anymore. I still attend meetings and review projects the firm is working on, but I'm no longer drawing.

I still enjoy lecturing, and over the past few years I've recorded notes for an autobiography I hope to write. I'm looking forward to the dedication ceremonies for the Pi Beta sorority house at USC. I've designed buildings for colleges across the country, but this is the first and only building I designed at my old school.

I've always tried to arrange my day with the toughest assignments in the first two thirds and the most pleasant in the last third. That way, I end my day on a positive note. I think I'll pick up some peppermint ice cream on the way home and surprise Della.

"My theory of the basics of urban planning is that people should be permitted to walk in the sunshine or shade and to shop or play in a controlled climate. The autos should travel and be contained at a lower level. Creating the environment is an important background for acceptance of change."

Remember Our Greatest Tool: Imagination

Spring 1973

My retirement dinner is tomorrow, and I find myself with mixed emotions. I wonder what my colleagues will remember about me. Will they think only of the public buildings that I've worked on? People seem to have changed, and residential architecture is less important. While I'll always treasure my work on such buildings as the Los Angeles County Courthouse, the Hall of Administration, the Federal Customs Building, and, of course, the airport, my favorites will always be the homes.

When you design a home for someone, it is the most important building they will ever build. You know how they say, "A man's home is his castle?" Well, it's true. I'd like to be remembered for the understated elegance that has made so many of my clients happy. People always ask why I love curves so much and incorporated them in so many designs — I don't really have an answer. I think I just adore graceful lines rather than squared-off edges. Sometimes it's a slight curve in a dining-room wall; sometimes the entire building is curved. I designed the Founder's Church of Religious Science in the round because the minister thought we shouldn't give the devil any corners to hide in!

I think of you, my grandson, as you embark on your greatest adventure. Here I am retiring just as you're graduating from law school and beginning

Opposite: *Satellite City, a visionary project that was never built.*

Paul R. Williams at age 53.

your career. I'm so proud of you. Seems like just yesterday you were a little boy, and I was telling you the story about the painters. Do you remember?

A paint contractor wanted to increase his business, so he came up with the idea of having all of his men dress in brand-new, pressed white overalls and arriving on the job a half hour early each day. Everyone in the neighborhood where they were working began to notice how neat and clean they were. Soon they were known as the cleanest, most efficient painters in town. Everyone wanted to hire them. After hearing that story, you insisted on getting dressed up to sell your school cookies. You probably sold more than anyone else. Now that I think about it, I suppose you're like me in that way. You have my quiet ways and shun unpleasantness. You also appreciate the importance of family and always help those wanting to learn. I've tried to teach you that success requires you to read, listen, and think. You must be doing something right, because you're off to Washington, D.C., to practice law.

I have probably waited too long to give you this notebook. I fear that you will think I'm disappointed because you didn't become an architect. I'll never be disappointed in you, or any of my grandchildren, if you just do your best and follow your heart. Perhaps the greatest legacy I can leave you is imagination. Remember, imagination can be a tool in creative problem solving. Use your imagination, and you'll never give up on finding solutions to problems, whatever they are.

Afterword
A Grandson Remembers...

Da—

While looking for material for a speech I'm to give to the Chamber of Commerce, I came across the notebook. As I began to read through the passages, I gained a greater understanding of Paul Williams, the architect, and the man. As our grandfather, you shielded us from the unpleasantness of your early career and the hardships of poverty. By example, you have given us the courage to face life's challenges. Los Angeles, and the world, have changed drastically in the years since your death in 1980.

People often ask why I didn't become an architect, but the bottom line is, I can't draw! You probably knew that long before you offered me a summer job in your office. I'm sure the other employees thought I was adopted, because I certainly didn't inherit your artistic skills.

I wasn't totally immune to your gifts. I do have an eye for art and design. Karen and I even designed the interior of Broadway Federal's Inglewood office. When selecting the color scheme, we remembered your telling us to always choose green if we couldn't decide on a color. You taught us that green comes in thousands of shades, and one has only to look at the leaves on a tree to understand the limitless possibilities. And you were right. Green is a color one doesn't tire of easily, because we have all grown up surrounded by Mother Nature's grasses, leaves, and flowers. We've learned to look at what we don't like about a situation and search for solutions — just as you did with design problems. I, too, plan my days with the toughest assignments first and try to end the day on a positive note. You'd be pleased that all of your grandchildren have incorporated imagination into our everyday lives. Cousin Gayle is a landscape designer and shares your love of flowers. Her brother Glenn is a loving father to his two little girls and has your entrepreneurial spirit. Karen can't draw, either, but expresses herself through photography and writing. She worked from your autobiographical notes and completed the biography you always wanted to write. Through your work, we have come to understand the importance of preservation and its impact on our history and culture.

In 1992, during the turmoil and civil unrest that rocked Los Angeles, we lost the headquarters of Broadway Federal Savings, a building of your design. As the buildings burned, I was flooded with emotions. And now, as the city rebuilds, I find a quote in your notes to inspire me. It's your definition of progress:

> "PROGRESS *is that you do something better today than the way you did it yesterday, and plan to do it even better tomorrow."*

If you were here we could go out and have a dish of ice cream to celebrate. Celebrate what, you ask? Well, maybe I didn't fall in love with architecture that summer almost thirty years ago, and I found out I didn't love being a lawyer, either. Remember the Midtown branch of Broadway Federal you designed—? Well, now I'm the president!

Even though you're no longer with us, know that I thank you. A gentle man with a dream, you have taught me by example that I can achieve my goals with *the will and the way.*

Your grandson,
Paul Claude

Paul C. Hudson, President, Broadway Federal Savings and Loan, *standing in front of the Midtown Office, Los Angeles.*

Bruce W. Talamon

58

Biographical Chronology

1894   Born February 18 at 842 Santee Street, Los Angeles, to Chester and Lila Williams, who died before his fifth birthday.

c.1900   Attended Sentuous Avenue Grammar School on Pico Boulevard. The only Negro in his class, he excelled in art and was encouraged to pursue a career in architecture by a local builder.

1912   Graduated from Polytechnic High School, Los Angeles.

1912–16   Attended Los Angeles School of Art and the Beaux Arts School of Design Atelier, winning the Beaux Arts Medal.

1913–15   Worked for Wilbur D. Cook, landscape architect, and learned to integrate the planning of house and garden. Gained experience in town planning.

1914   At age 20, won first prize of $200 for design for a neighborhood civic center in Pasadena, California.

1915   Certified as an architect.
Awarded first honorable mention in architecture at the Chicago Emancipation Celebration.

1916–19   Attended the University of Southern California as one of eight students studying architectural engineering.
Worked for Reginald Johnson, and worked on first design of a home over $100,000. Gained experience in fine home design.

1917   Married Della Mae Givens, June 27.

1920–22 Worked for John C. Austin and gained experience in large public buildings. Assisted in the preparation of construction drawings of the Shrine Auditorium and the First Methodist Church, among others.

1920–28 Appointed to the first City Planning Commission of Los Angeles.

1921 Licensed to practice architecture in California.

1922 Established his own firm, Paul R. Williams and Associates, with offices in the Stock Exchange Building.

1923 Became first African-American member of the American Institute of Architects (AIA) by joining the Southern California Chapter.

1927 Moved office to Wilshire Arts Building, Los Angeles.

1929 Appointed to National Monuments Committee by President Coolidge.

1933–41 Appointed to first Los Angeles Housing Commission by Mayor Frank Shaw.

1936–54 Member, Metropolitan Los Angeles YMCA, board of directors.

1936 Licensed to practice in Washington, D.C.

1939 Award of Merit, Southern California Chapter AIA, for Music Corporation of America Building, Beverly Hills, 1937.

1941 Honorary doctor of science degree, Lincoln University, Missouri. Omega Psi Phi, national award. Opened office in Bogotá, Colombia.

c.1942 Architect, U.S. Navy, World War II.

Music Corporation of America Building, 1937.

1945	Published first book, *Small Homes of Tomorrow.*
1946	Published second book, *New Homes for Today.*
1947	Became vice-president and director of Broadway Federal Savings and Loan, the oldest federal African-American savings and loan west of the Mississippi.
	Designed unit of Los Angeles General Hospital—the first time an African-American had been selected to design a large public building in Los Angeles.

Williams receiving the Spingarn Medal from Senator W. Stuart Symington, St. Louis, Missouri, 1953.

1948	Veterans of Foreign Wars Award of Merit, civil architecture.
	Licensed to practice in New York.
1949–55	Member, California Housing Commission, appointed by Governor Earl Warren.
1951	Distinguished Service Award, National Conference of Christians and Jews, Builders and Trades Committee.
	Office relocated to 3757 Wilshire Boulevard, Los Angeles, employing 52 people.
1952	Honorary doctor of architecture degree, Howard University, Washington, D.C. Presentation made by President Truman.
	Delegate to Republican National Convention, Chicago.
1953	Member, National Housing Commission, appointed by President Eisenhower.
	Awarded NAACP Spingarn Medal for contributions to his profession.
1953–65	Member, Municipal Art Commission, serving as president for eleven years.
1954	Chairman, AIA Competitions Committee.

1956	Honorary doctor of fine arts degree, awarded by Tuskegee Institute.
1957	Elected to the AIA College of Fellows, becoming the first African-American to be honored.
1957	Los Angeles Chamber of Commerce Award for Creative Planning.
c.1960	President, Advisory Committee of State of California, U.S. Commission on Civil Rights.
1961	Presentation of Paul R. Williams portrait to Howard University on the occasion of the golden anniversary of the School of Engineering and Architecture. In association with Hilyard Robinson, designed the new Engineering and Architecture Building at Howard.
1960	Licensed to practice in Tennessee. Delegate to Republican National Convention.
1964	Honorary doctor of fine arts degree, Atlanta University. Licensed to practice in Nevada.
1973	Retired. Commendation, AIA/LA Chapter. Minority Architects and Planners Award.
1977	City Council Commendation for artistic contributions to Los Angeles.
1980	Died January 23, Los Angeles, California.

City Councilman Tom Bradley, who would later become Mayor of Los Angeles, presents Williams with City Commendation, 1965.

Glossary

American Institute of Architects (AIA): A national organization of architects, founded in 1857. Current membership: 56,000, including 1700 Fellows.

Marian Anderson (1902–1993): A contralto opera singer who, in 1955, was the first African-American woman to sing at the Metropolitan Opera.

Architecture: The art and science of designing and constructing buildings.

Beaux-Arts style: A nineteenth century revival of classical building styles, named after the Ecole des Beaux-Arts, an academy of fine arts and architecture in Paris, France.

City planning: To outline or plan the design and future growth of a city.

Client: A person who hires the professional services of another.

Commission: The granting of authority by a client to carry out a particular task.

Contractor: One who agrees to furnish materials and perform certain building construction services for a fee.

Design: A drawing, pattern, or sketch for something that is to be built; or, to create an object according to such a plan. It may also refer to a decorative pattern or an arrangement of objects.

Frederick Douglass (1817–1895): An African-American abolitionist and journalist.

Drafting table: A slanted table where an architect or draftsman makes drawings.

Engineering: The application of scientific and mathematical principles to practical ends, such as design and construction.

English Tudor style: Characteristic of an architectural style from the Tudor Period (1485–1693) of English history, featuring exposed beams.

Facade: The face of a building, usually the exterior front.

Firm: A commercial partnership of two or more people.

Fixtures: Something attached as a permanent part of a building, furnishing it with utilities, such as plumbing or lighting.

Floor plan: A scale diagram of a room or building drawn as if seen from above.

Housing project: A publicly-funded and administered housing development, usually for low-income families.

Interior design: The planning and layout, decoration, and furnishings of the inside of a building or home.

"Jim Crow" Laws: Laws that promoted the segregation of African-Americans.

Landscape: To adorn or improve a section of ground by grading, clearing, or planting.

License: A legal document stating that an architect is qualified to build in that state or community.

Modern architecture: The style of architecture characterized by cubic shapes, lighter mass, and the use of materials such as glass, concrete, and steel.

The National Association for the Advancement of Colored People (NAACP): This organization was founded in 1909 to fight for the rights of African-Americans.

Preservation: Protecting buildings from loss, damage, decay, or demolition.

Rendering: An artist's drawing or painting of how a building is going to look.

Jackie Robinson (1919–1972): The first African-American to play major-league baseball. He played for the Brooklyn Dodgers.

Site: The land upon which something is built.

Style: To design, arrange, or decorate something guided by a prevailing or historical mode, custom, or fashion.

Technology: The use of science for practical purposes, especially in engineering and industry.

Booker T. Washington (1856–1915): An African-American educator and author.

Williams with draftsman.